ARKANSAS

States

by Jason Kirchner

CAPSTONE PRESS
a capstone imprint

Next Page Books are published by Capstone Press,
1710 Roe Crest Drive, North Mankato, Minnesota 56003
www.mycapstone.com

Library of Congress Cataloging-in-Publication Data
Cataloging-in-publication information is on file with the Library of
Congress.
ISBN 978-1-5157-0390-7 (library binding)
ISBN 978-1-5157-0450-8 (paperback)
ISBN 978-1-5157-0502-4 (ebook PDF)

Editorial Credits
Jaclyn Jaycox, editor; Richard Korab and Katy LaVigne, designers;
Morgan Walters, media researcher; Laura Manthe, production specialist

Photo Credits
Capstone Press: Angi Gahler, map 4, 7; Corbis: AS400 DB, 26;
Dreamstime: Reddogs, bottom left 21; Getty Images: Interim Archives,
12, 25, PhotoQuest, 27, Wesley Hitt, 9; Newscom: REUTERS/Jim
Young, bottom 18, ZUMA Press/Robin Nelson, middle 18, ZUMApress/
The Commercial Appeal, middle 19; One Mile Up, Inc., flag, seal 23;
Shutterstock: Bildagentur Zoonar GmbH, bottom 24, BluIz60, top
left 21, Daniel Prudek, bottom right 20, Debby Wong, top 19, Everett
Historical, bottom 19, Henryk Sadura, 5, IrinaK, bottom 8, 14, 16,
Jason L. Price, 10, Jill Nightingale, bottom left 20, Joseph Sohm,
13, kanusommer, top right 20, Kathleen Struckle, 11, Khakimullin
Aleksandr, top right 21, michaeljung, 15, mnapoli, cover, Pekka
Nikonen, bottom right 21, Ross Ellet, 6, Rudmer Zwerver, top 24,
SergeyIT, top left 20, stocklight, top 18, Tarasyuk Igor, middle right
21, Tom Reichner, middle 21, Zack Frank, 7, bottom left 8; SuperStock:
Everett Collection, 28; Wikimedia: FEMA Photo Library, 29

All design elements by Shutterstock

Printed and bound in China.
0316/CA21600187
012016   009436F16

TABLE OF CONTENTS

Want to take your research further? Ask your librarian if your school subscribes to PebbleGo Next. If so, when you see this helpful symbol ⟨⟩ throughout the book, log onto www.pebblegonext.com for bonus downloads and information.

LOCATION

Arkansas lies in the south-central United States. The Mississippi River forms most of its eastern border. Across the river to the east are Tennessee and Mississippi. To the north is Missouri. Across the southern border is Louisiana. Oklahoma and Texas lie to the west. Little Rock, the state capital, is in the center of the state. Little Rock is also Arkansas' largest city. The state's next largest cities are Fort Smith, Fayetteville, and Springdale.

PebbleGo Next Bonus! To print and label your own map, go to www.pebblegonext.com and search keywords:

AR MAP

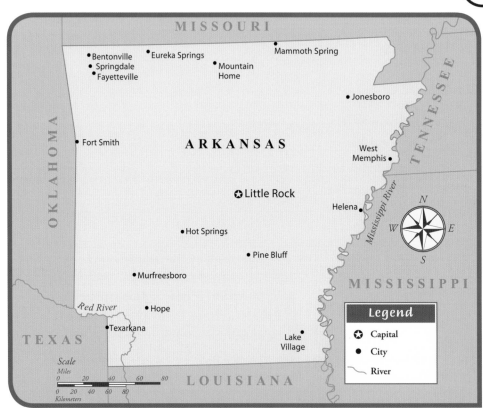

Little Rock sits on the banks of the Arkansas River and has a population of almost 200,000.

GEOGRAPHY

Arkansas has two landscapes. Hills and mountains in northwestern and west-central Arkansas are called the highlands. The flat lowlands cover the rest of the state. The Ozark Plateau covers northwest Arkansas. Within these forested hills are valleys, lakes, and streams. The Ouachita Mountains reach into western Arkansas from Oklahoma. Mount Magazine lies north of these mountains. It is the highest point in the state, rising 2,753 feet (839 meters) above sea level. The Arkansas River Valley cuts between the Ozark and Ouachita ranges. Fertile plains cover eastern Arkansas. Southwest Arkansas has thick pine forests.

PebbleGo Next Bonus! To watch a video about the Museum of the Arkansas Grand Prairie, go to www.pebblegonext.com and search keywords:

AR VIDEO

Spirits Creek is one of the highlights of the Ozark Highlands Trail.

Mount Magazine State Park is located on Mount Magazine. It covers over 2,200 acres (890 hectares).

Pea Ridge National Military Park

Bull Shoals Lake

Norfork Lake

Mammoth Spring

Beaver Lake

OZARK PLATEAU

BOSTON MOUNTAINS

CROWLEY'S RIDGE

St. Francis River

ARKANSAS RIVER VALLEY

White River

Mount Magazine

OUACHITA MOUNTAINS

Hot Springs National Park

Arkansas River

MISSISSIPPI ALLUVIAL PLAIN

Lake Ouachita

Mississippi River

Red River

Ouachita River

WEST GULF COASTAL PLAIN

Lake Chicot

Legend

▲ Highest Point

Lake

Mountain Range

National Park

○ Point of Interest

River

Scale

Miles
0   20   40   60   80

Kilometers
0   20   40   60   80

WEATHER

Arkansas has a mild climate. The state's average winter temperature is 42 degrees Fahrenheit (6 degrees Celsius). Summers are warm, with an average temperature of 79°F (26°C).

Average High and Low Temperatures (Little Rock, AR)

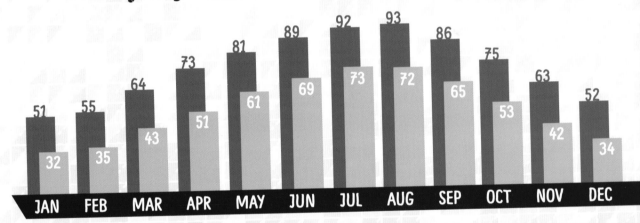

	JAN	FEB	MAR	APR	MAY	JUN	JUL	AUG	SEP	OCT	NOV	DEC
High	51	55	64	73	81	89	92	93	86	75	63	52
Low	32	35	43	51	61	69	73	72	65	53	42	34

LANDMARKS

Pea Ridge

Pea Ridge battlefield in northwestern Arkansas is the site of a fierce Civil War battle. Today it is the most intact Civil War battlefield in the country. The military park spans 4,300 acres (1,740 hectares) and includes a section of the Cherokee Trail of Tears. This was the trail the Cherokee Indians followed to Oklahoma when they were forced to move from their eastern homelands.

Blanchard Springs Caverns

Blanchard Springs Caverns in northern Arkansas is a cave system with some of the world's most spectacular rock formations. Minerals and dripping water combine to create colored limestone formations. Visitors camp, picnic, and swim nearby.

Eureka Springs

    Eureka Springs is a Victorian resort town in the Ozark Mountains in northwest Arkansas. Shops, art galleries, museums, spas, historic hotels, and festivals attract tourists to the small town.

René-Robert Cavelier claimed land, including Arkansas, for his home country of France in 1682.

American Indians lived in Arkansas thousands of years ago. In 1541 Spanish explorer Hernando de Soto led the first Europeans to Arkansas. French explorers Jacques Marquette and Louis Jolliet arrived in Arkansas in 1673. In 1682 René-Robert Cavelier claimed the Mississippi River Valley, including present-day Arkansas, for France. He named the area Louisiana. The United States bought Louisiana from France in 1803. The sale was called the Louisiana Purchase. In 1819 Arkansas became a territory, and in 1836 Arkansas became the 25th state.

Arkansas' government has three branches. The governor is the leader of the executive branch, which carries out laws. The legislature is made up of a 35-member Senate and a 100-member House of Representatives. They make the laws for Arkansas. The judicial branch is made up of judges and courts. They uphold the laws.

Arkansas' state capitol building is located in Little Rock.

INDUSTRY

Arkansas' economy is tied to its natural resources. About 40 percent of its land is farmed. Arkansas farmers grow cotton, soybeans, hay, and sorghum. Arkansas is the nation's top producer of rice. It is also a top producer of broilers, which are young chickens. Trees are used to make paper products. Textile factories weave cotton into cloth. Natural gas is the state's leading mined product. Arkansas also mines coal and oil. Arkansas relies on its natural beauty, mountains, and rivers to support tourism. The state has more than 50 state parks.

Arkansas produces 49 percent of the rice in the United States.

Service jobs make up Arkansas' largest industry. More than 75 percent of Arkansas workers have service jobs such as teachers, sales clerks, and insurance agents.

One of Arkansas' leading service industries is retail.

POPULATION

Most Arkansans have European backgrounds. In the 1800s British, German, Irish, and Dutch people settled in Arkansas. Today more than 2 million of the state's people are white.

Arkansas also has a large African-American population. Nearly one-half million African-Americans live in Arkansas. Most African-Americans are descended from slaves who worked on farms and plantations before the Civil War.

Population by Ethnicity

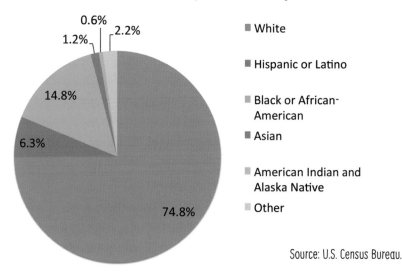

0.6%
1.2%
2.2%
14.8%
6.3%
74.8%

- White
- Hispanic or Latino
- Black or African-American
- Asian
- American Indian and Alaska Native
- Other

Source: U.S. Census Bureau.

Hispanics are the state's fastest growing ethnic group. The state's Hispanic population includes more than 185,000 people.

At one time Arkansas had a large American Indian population. Today a small number of Indians live in Arkansas, mainly in the northwest. About 35,000 Asians live in Arkansas. Many came to the state in the 1970s and 1980s from Southeast Asia.

FAMOUS PEOPLE

Bill Clinton (1946–) was the 42nd U.S. president from 1993 to 2001. Before becoming president, he was governor of Arkansas for 12 years. He was born in Hope.

Sam Walton (1918–1992), a Newport native, founded the Walmart chain of stores. He opened the first one in Bentonville. Today Walmart is the biggest retailer in the United States.

Maya Angelou (1928–2014) was a poet and novelist. Her best-known work is *I Know Why the Caged Bird Sings*. She was raised in St. Louis, Missouri, and Stamps, Arkansas.

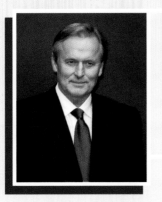

John Grisham (1955–) is a popular author. Many of his books have been made into movies, including *The Firm* and *The Client*. He was born in Jonesboro.

Daisy Bates (1914–1999) led the National Association for the Advancement of Colored People (NAACP) during the fight to integrate Little Rock's schools in 1957. She was born in Huttig.

Douglas MacArthur (1880–1964) was the commander of Allied forces in the Southwest Pacific region during World War II. He was born in Little Rock.

STATE SYMBOLS

Tree

pine

Flower

apple blossom

Bird

mockingbird

Insect

honeybee

PebbleGo Next Bonus! To make a sweet treat using Arkansas' leading crop, go to www.pebblegonext.com and search keywords:
AR RECIPE

Folk Dance

square dance

Musical Instrument

fiddle

Mammal

white-tailed deer

Beverage

milk

Rock

bauxite

Mineral

quartz crystal

21

FAST FACTS

STATEHOOD
1836

CAPITAL ☆
Little Rock

LARGEST CITY •
Little Rock

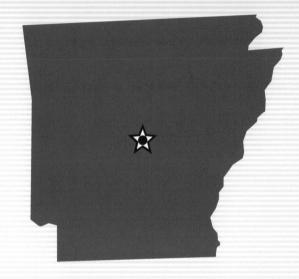

SIZE
52,035 square miles (134,770 square kilometers) land area
(2010 U.S. Census Bureau)

POPULATION
2,959,373 (2013 U.S. Census estimate)

STATE NICKNAME
Natural State

STATE MOTTO
"Regnat Populus," which is Latin for "The People Rule"

STATE SEAL

Arkansas' state seal was adopted in 1864. The seal shows an eagle holding a banner in its beak. The state motto, "Regnat Populus," is written on the banner. An angel of mercy and a sword of justice are on either side of the eagle. Above them is the goddess of liberty. A shield has pictures of a steamboat, a plow, a beehive, and wheat. These pictures stand for Arkansas' natural resources.

PebbleGo Next Bonus! To print and color your own flag, go to www.pebblegonext.com and search keywords:

AR FLAG

STATE FLAG

The Arkansas flag has a white diamond with a blue border on a red background. The diamond stands for the state's diamond mines. Within the blue border are 25 white stars. They stand for Arkansas' place as the 25th state. In the center of the diamond is the state's name surrounded by four blue stars. The blue star at the top stands for the Confederacy. The three stars in the lower half of the diamond represent Spain, France, and the United States. These three countries have ruled Arkansas.

MINING PRODUCTS

natural gas

MANUFACTURED GOODS

computer and electronic
equipment, petroleum and coal
products, chemicals, food products,
transportation equipment,
fabricated metal products,
machinery

FARM PRODUCTS

chickens, hogs, catfish, eggs,
rice, soybeans, apples, grapes,
peaches, cotton

PebbleGo Next Bonus!
To learn the lyrics to
the state song, go to
www.pebblegonext.com
and search keywords:

AR SONG

ARKANSAS TIMELINE

1500s
Caddo, Osage, and Quapaw Indians are living in present-day Arkansas when European explorers arrive.

1541
Spanish explorer Hernando de Soto passes through Arkansas.

1620
The Pilgrims establish a colony in the New World in present-day Massachusetts.

1673
French explorers Jacques Marquette and Louis Jolliet travel down the Mississippi River and stop at the mouth of the Arkansas River.

1682 René-Robert Cavelier, known as Sieur de La Salle, claims the Mississippi River Valley, including present-day Arkansas, for France.

1686 French explorers build Arkansas' first settlement, Arkansas Post, in eastern Arkansas.

1803 The United States buys the Louisiana Territory, including present-day Arkansas, from France. The sale is called the Louisiana Purchase.

1819 Arkansas Territory is created.

1836 Arkansas becomes the 25th U.S. state on June 15.

1861   Arkansas leaves the United States to join a new country called the Confederate States of America.

1861–1865   The Union and the Confederacy fight the Civil War. Arkansas fights for the Confederacy. Key battles are fought in Arkansas during the Civil War.

1868   Arkansas rejoins the Union.

1914–1918   World War I is fought; the United States enters the war in 1917.

1932   Hattie Caraway of Arkansas is the first woman elected to the U.S. Senate.

1939–1945   World War II is fought; the United States enters the war in 1941.

1957   Troops are sent to Central High School in Little Rock to enforce a court order requiring schools to include students of all races. The troops make sure African-American students are able to safely enter the school.

1978   Bill Clinton is elected governor of Arkansas for the first time.

1992 Americans elect former Arkansas governor Bill Clinton as president. He is elected president again in 1996.

2007 A tornado hits Dumas in eastern Arkansas, injuring several people and damaging dozens of homes and businesses.

2011 The lower Mississippi River in the central United States floods in April and May due to heavy rains. The flooding causes billions of dollars in damages.

2015 A woman finds an 8.52-carat diamond in Crater of Diamonds State Park; it is the 5th-largest diamond found by a park visitor since 1972.

Glossary

descend *(dee-SEND)*—to belong to a later generation of the same family

ethnic *(ETH-nik)*—related to a group of people and their culture

executive *(ig-ZE-kyuh-tiv)*—the branch of government that makes sure laws are followed

fierce *(FEERSS)*—daring and dangerous

formation *(for-MAY-shuhn)*—a pattern or a shape

industry *(IN-duh-stree)*—a business which produces a product or provides a service

integrate *(IN-tuh-grate)*—to bring people of different races together in schools and other public places

legislature *(LEJ-iss-lay-chur)*—a group of elected officials who have the power to make or change laws for a country or state

petroleum *(puh-TROH-lee-uhm)*—an oily liquid found below the earth's surface used to make gasoline, heating oil, and many other products

plantation *(plan-TAY-shuhn)*—a large farm found in warm areas; before the Civil War, plantations in the South used slave labor

plateau *(pla-TOH)*—an area of high, flat land

region *(REE-juhn)*—a large area

Read More

Bailer, Darice. *What's Great About Arkansas?* Our Great States. Minneapolis: Lerner Publications, 2014.

Ganeri, Anita. *United States of America: A Benjamin Blog and His Inquisitive Dog Guide.* Country Guides. Chicago: Heinemann Raintree, 2015.

King, David. *Arkansas.* It's My State! New York: Cavendish Square Publishing, 2014.

Internet Sites

FactHound offers a safe, fun way to find Internet sites related to this book. All of the sites on FactHound have been researched by our staff.

Here's all you do:

Visit *www.facthound.com*

Type in this code: 9781515703907

 Check out projects, games and lots more at
www.capstonekids.com

Critical Thinking Using the Common Core

1. Northwestern Arkansas includes a section of the Cherokee Trail of Tears. This was a trail the Cherokee Indians followed when they were forced to move from their homelands. How would you feel if you had to move, but didn't want to? (Integration of Knowledge and Ideas)

2. Farming is an important part of Arkansas' economy. What kinds of crops are grown here? (Key Ideas and Details)

3. In 1957 troops were sent to Little Rock to enforce a court order that required schools to include students of all races. Why do you think troops were needed? (Integration of Knowledge and Ideas)

Index